curriculum

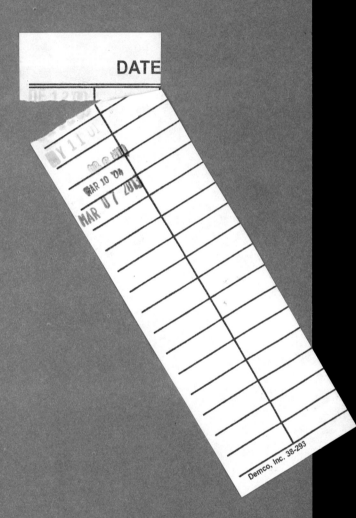

DATE

MAY 11 0
MAR 10 '04
MAR 07 20

Demco, Inc. 38-293

For all
boys and girls
who like
Indians and Animals

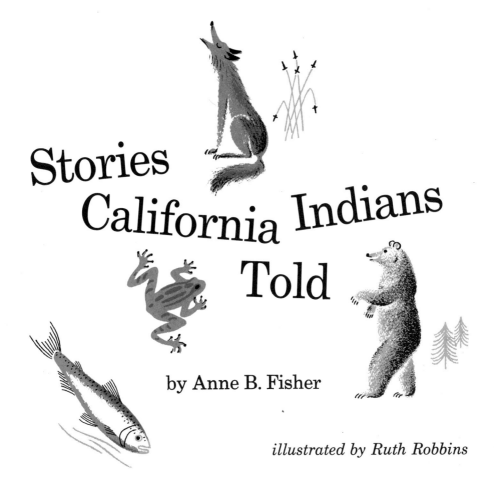

Stories California Indians Told

by Anne B. Fisher

illustrated by Ruth Robbins

CALIFORNIA STATE SERIES

published by

CALIFORNIA STATE DEPARTMENT OF EDUCATION

Sacramento, 1965

printed in
CALIFORNIA OFFICE OF STATE PRINTING
SACRAMENTO   1 ST PRINT   45M   1965

Foreword

The California Indian stories in this book are authentic. Most of the myths were collected by the famous early anthropologist and naturalist, Dr. C. Hart Merriam who wrote the tales down just as they were told to him by Indian story-tellers. Dr. Merriam then related the myths to the author who turned them into stories for children and young people. In these stories the author has kept the true spirit of Indian life such as it was long ago in California.

Because such stories have been preserved, both young and old can have a better appreciation of the rich creative thought and varied cultural settings of California's first dwellers.

As the map in this book shows, California was divided into three main regions. Though hunting, fishing, and gathering acorns were done everywhere, each of these regions very early developed its own way of life and came to be recognized as a separate culture area.

In the northwest along the coast and around the Klamath River there dwelled the Yurok, Karok, and Hupa Indians. Here were the great salmon fishermen, distinguished by their redwood plank houses, their great river boats carved by the stone and bone adze, elk antlers shaped into beautiful spoons, and the most delicate baskets twined into waterproof containers and hats. These and other artistic achievements show the ancient connections of the Indians of this area with the totem pole Indians of the Pacific Northwest.

Along the coast and river-entwined valley reaching from Mt. Shasta in the north to Tehachapi in the south was the central hearth of California Indian culture. Living in small harmonious villages were the Shasta, Pomo, Maidu, Miwok, Yokuts and many other Indian peoples. Nature provided an almost endless variety of food and the Indians here developed the techniques of harvest and food preparation. Out of this region came the world's greatest basket weavers.

In the third area, around the Channel Islands and from Santa Barbara south to Los Angeles lived the Chumash and Gabrielino Indians. These were the artistic carvers of soapstone objects and the builders of massive plank canoes. Whereas they looked to the sea for much of their food, other groups toward the east, like the Diegueño and the Cahuilla of the interior were true desert dwellers baking the mescal root in earth ovens and boiling the mesquite beans in graceful pottery containers. On the Colorado River were the Yumas and Mohave, cultivators of corn, beans, and squash, a practice acquired from their southwest Indian neighbors.

In these myths you will find that some of the characters and animals do things that appear to be impossible. California Indians, like all other people, were imaginative and attempted to explain in their myths the world of nature around them. Animals, reptiles, or insects were often given the ability to think and speak like humans and to exert almost unlimited physical powers. Yet these stories were very real to Indian children and adults, as real as our own legendary tales are to us.

Adan E. Treganza

Associate Professor of Anthropology
San Francisco State College
San Francisco, California

Editor's Note
Dr. C. Hart Merriam preferred his own spelling of California Indian tribal names. For example, he called one of the Indian tribes living in the central area of California MEWUK, *instead of* MIWOK *as the name is usually spelled today. In these stories we have used the spelling of tribal names that is in common use.*

Contents

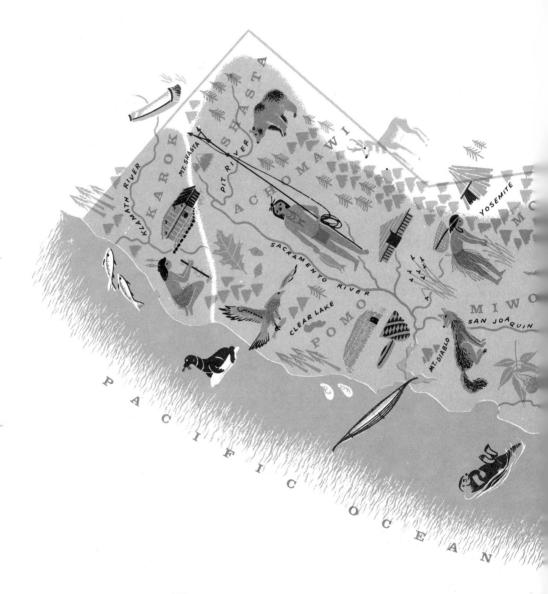

This is how the Indians of California lived
when these stories were told

How California Was Made

Long ago, the Medicine Man of the Gabrielino Indians far down in the southern part of California, stood watching the leaves fall. He looked around at the brown hills. He heard the wind rustling the rushes and poles of the Indian huts. Medicine Man smiled and turned toward his own hut. The time for story telling was here.

Inside his hut, he carefully painted red and white stripes on his body. The red was as bright as the toyon berries that grew on the hillsides. The white was like snow on distant mountain peaks.

Next, Medicine Man took his story-telling headdress from its place among his medicine bags and magic charms. The headdress was like a hair net, made from the tough strands of the milkweed plant. Medicine Man pulled the net over his black hair. Through the net, the soft down from baby eagles' breasts had been drawn. The pale eagle feathers fluffed out from the meshes to make a fuzzy cap.

When Medicine Man, whom the Indians called the *Shaman*, was ready, he went outside and called in a loud voice to the Indians:

"Come sit around the fire and I will tell you a story."

From all the huts around, the Indian men and their wives and the Indian boys and girls came running. The people loved stories and they loved Medicine Man to tell them. One by one they settled down by the crackling fire. The fire gleamed in their eyes as they listened to the story Medicine Man told.

Before the time of people on earth, Medicine Man told them, *Kwawar*, the Great Spirit, looked down from his place in the sky. There was no earth to look at, but only water. There were no trees, no mountains, no valleys. The Great Spirit looked at all the water and he made up his mind: he would make land where things could grow.

"But how shall I make land?" he asked himself, looking straight off into the sky. "I don't have a single thing to use as a beginning."

He looked down again. There, suddenly, he saw a giant turtle in the water. The turtle was so huge it was as big as an island. The Great Spirit had forgotten about Turtle because he had made turtles such a long time before.

"I'll make land on the back of Turtle," he decided.

But Turtle, huge though he was, was not big enough to make the beautiful land later called California.

He thought and thought what to do. Then an idea popped into his head.

He called down, "Turtle! Hurry and bring all six of your brothers here where I can talk to them."

Turtle went swimming off. It took him a whole day to find his first brother. Then another day to find the second one. Finally, at the end of six days, he had found them all.

"The Great Spirit wants you," he told them and led his six brothers back to where the Great Spirit waited. Each of Turtle's brothers was as big as he. Floating all together in one place, they were like seven great islands.

The Great Spirit nodded. The seven turtles all floating in one spot were big enough to hold up the new land he planned to create.

"Now, Turtle Brothers," the Great Spirit called down, "form a long line head to tail — a line running north and south. You three to the south move toward the east a bit."

The Turtle Brothers did as they were told.

The Great Spirit was very pleased. "You'll make a wonderful California!" he told them. "Now, stay just where you are in the water. You must always stay very, very quiet just where you are, because this is a great honor I have given you — to bear California on your backs."

The Turtle Brothers obeyed and stayed very still.

"Now for some land where things can grow," Great Spirit murmured. He took some tules (rushes) from his supply in the sky and spread them rather thickly over the backs of Turtle Brothers. Then he scooped up some earth from his giant pile and spread it over the tules and patted it down well.

"These humps on the Turtle Brothers' backs will make good mountains," he said to himself.

When the soil was all patted down he wiped his hands on a clean white cloud and decided what to do next.

"Trees!" he cried. "I need some trees to grow."

He stuck his fingers into the earth on the Turtle

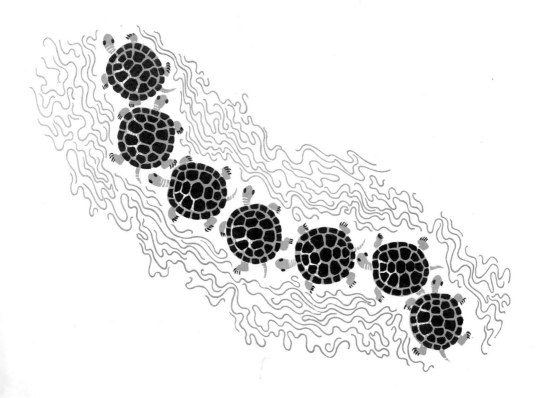

Brothers' backs and made trees grow. Then he let a little water seep up between the edges of the turtles' shells to make lakes. Water from the lakes leaked over the earth covering the turtles' backs and made rivers. The rivers ran down into the sea at the west side.

The Great Spirit studied what he had made and frowned. Everything was too quiet in the new world.

"That won't do," said the Great Spirit. "I need birds to sing." He picked some leaves from the new trees, blew on them and they flew away singing and turned into birds.

The Great Spirit smiled, looking at the new land and the mountains and the rivers he had made. He looked at the young trees rustling their leaves. He listened to the music of the birds, and he turned away satisfied.

Then came trouble. The giant Turtle Brothers began to get restless. They wanted to swim away.

"I want to swim east," said one.

"No!" snapped another, "west is better. West is where the sun sets. I've always wanted to see where the sun goes down."

For days and days, the Turtle Brothers kept quarreling among themselves. They just couldn't agree.

One day four swam east and three swam west!

"Ga—rumble," went the earth under California. The ground trembled and split with a grinding noise. A crack opened in the earth, zigzagging among the trees. The trees shuddered and their roots twisted. Birds fled into the sky where they wheeled and screeched in fear.

Suddenly, the earth shaking ceased. The giant turtles stopped swimming away from each other. All the tules and earth that the Great Spirit had piled on their backs was too heavy to carry far. Also, the land was so packed and hardened that it held them back. They could only swim the width of the crack in the earth. There was nothing to do but try to make peace among themselves. They made peace and the earth stopped shaking.

But even now, every once in a while, the Turtle Brothers that hold up California start quarreling among themselves again. Each time, the ground shakes and the trees quiver. Sometimes, the huts of Indians and buildings of white men go down. A crack splits through the earth. Then, when Turtle Brothers make peace, everything becomes quiet once more.

At times, even the sky where the Great Spirit lives shakes. But this is not because of the Turtle Brothers fighting among themselves. It is because people are fighting. When people on earth fight each other, there is a great shudder in the land above the clouds. The clouds crack open and the Great Spirit looks down through the crack. He grows very sad when he sees men quarreling.

This is the story Medicine Man told to his people, the Gabrielinos. The Gabrielinos knew that it was true because they could see the mountains and hills and rivers running over the humps of the seven Turtle Brothers. There the turtles were, underneath all, floating head to tail from the north of California to the south.

As the Indians listened to their *Shaman* around the campfire, they hoped that Turtle Brothers would not start quarreling and make the earth quake. And they hoped that there would be no fights among themselves, for each Gabrielino knew that it was bad luck to fight each other and shake the home of the Great Spirit.

How Coyote Helped to
Light the World

This is the story told by Medicine Man of the Southern Pomos, about how light came into the world.

A long time ago when the world was very young and there was not a single beam of light anywhere, a hawk kept flying around trying to find his way in the black sky.

Down on the black earth, Coyote was stumbling around trying to find his way. Day after day, Coyote groped through the thick darkness trying to find a ray of light somewhere.

Above, Hawk flew around and around trying to find his way to light.

At last, Coyote groped and stumbled and pulled his way up a high mountain. In the darkness he bumped into trees and rocks. He skinned his haunches. He fell. He skidded backward, but he kept on going. His paws got very sore, throbbing with each step upward, but he finally reached the top.

Just then Hawk happened to swoop lower and lower over the very same mountain.

"Bang!" Hawk flew too low and bumped right into Coyote and bent his whiskers and hit his nose.

"Yeao—ouh!" howled Coyote in the dark. He clapped his paws to his face and rubbed his nose.

"Squaw—eek!" screamed Hawk in the dark as he shook his feathers straight.

But Hawk and Coyote didn't get angry and fight.

Hawk said to Coyote, "I'm sorry I hit you, but it is dark and I can't see. You nearly scared the feathers off me."

"That was not your fault, Hawk," said Coyote. "I couldn't see either, or I would have kept my long nose out of your way. You nearly scared me out of my skin."

With that, Hawk flew above Coyote and hung fluttering in the darkness and talked about how wonderful it would be if there were light in the world. Coyote sat on his haunches on the cold mountain top and talked back about light, too.

Then Coyote began to think. "It doesn't do any good for you to fly around talking to me about the dark, Hawk," he said with a sigh. "And it doesn't do me any good to sit here on my haunches and grumble in the dark."

"You are right," Hawk told him. "But what can we do, a hawk and a coyote?"

Coyote was silent, thinking hard. Hawk grew silent too, except for the fluttering sound of his wings. But the harder Hawk and Coyote thought, the darker it seemed.

Then, when Coyote stopped thinking so hard and pricked up his ears and listened to the whispering darkness, an idea came.

"I'll gather a heap of tules from the marsh," he told Hawk, "and roll them into a ball with my paws."

"How can you get light from a ball of tules?" Hawk asked. "Tules are just marsh grasses." He sniffed aloud in a great big "Sniff-er!" Then he flew away in disgust.

Coyote felt very much alone as he stumbled down the night-covered mountain to the marsh and gathered tules that grew there. His front paws ached and grew raw from pulling tules. He told himself that light was worth sore paws and a weary back. He kept on working until he had a big pile of tules beside him.

He picked up one of the long stems of grass and wadded it into a small ball. Then he wrapped another tule around that, pulling it very tight so it would be solid. He kept on doing this until he had a very big solid ball, a ball bigger than had ever been made in all the world, before.

All this took lots of time. Hawk grew lonely and flew back to be near Coyote in the dark. He was guided by the sound of the tules that rattled while Coyote wadded and twisted them together.

"I'm sorry I flew away," said Hawk. "I'll help you any way I can—if you think you can bring light to the world."

"Well, it's about time," Coyote snorted. "I've worked alone and I need help if we are ever to have light."

Coyote felt around in the dark and Hawk felt around in the dark until they touched each other.

"Here," said Coyote, and he gave the big, round bundle of tules to Hawk. He groped around on the mountain top and found some pieces of flint. These he handed to Hawk, too.

"Now what do I do?" asked Hawk, still not believing that he, a bird, could help bring light to all the world.

"Take the tule ball in your claws and the flints in your beak and fly as high as you can," Coyote told him in a sure voice. "Way up there where only you can fly, strike the flints together, make a spark and light the ball of tule. Then leave the burning ball and fly away as fast as you can before you catch on fire."

Hawk was pleased because he could fly and Coyote couldn't. He took the tule ball and the flints and strained every muscle in his wings to fly higher than he had ever flown before. He'd show Coyote how high he could go!

"Whoosh" he went up higher and higher, while Coyote called out "Ye-ou—ooo" to cheer him on.

Up and up Hawk went, so high that the "Ye-ou—oos" of Coyote cheering him on grew fainter and fainter. Finally, he was so high that he couldn't even hear Coyote's calls. There was only silence and blackness and the rushing sound of Hawk's great, climbing wings.

"Now I'll light the tules" Hawk said to himself. "It's time because now I'm so high up there's hardly any air to beat my wings against."

He worked with his claws and his beak to strike the flints together for a spark. It was hard because he had to hold onto the big tule ball and keep his wings spread wide on the thin air.

A bright, hot spark suddenly flew up from the flints! Hawk's wings lashed the air in excitement.

But just at that instant North Wind discovered Hawk and went "Whe-e-on" very hard. "Get out of here," North Wind hissed. "Up here is where I live! Not even a hawk is allowed up here!" The spark died.

North Wind "We-e-e-oned" so hard that Hawk could scarcely hold onto the huge tule ball. His tail feathers were blown back and fourth until he was afraid they would be ripped off. The feathers on the back of his head blew forward into his eyes.

Hawk was discouraged, but he was proud. He wouldn't let Coyote down there on earth think that he couldn't do his part in lighting the world.

He worked harder than ever in spite of North Wind. He gripped the tule ball firmly in his sharp claws; then he wedged one of the flints just under one claw. The other

20

flint he held in his beak. He struck them together many, many times. Just when he had almost lost hope, a new dancing spark leaped into life!

Swiftly, Hawk touched the spark to the bundle of tules. The spark caught. Red and yellow flames licked upward around the great ball. Suddenly, the whole ball blazed with so much light and heat that Hawk's joy turned to fear. He let go and went racing downward.

Even as he flew down to the cooler air, he was filled with a sense of wonder at the giant ball of flame he had left blazing there above. Light poured over the whole sky until Hawk felt almost blinded from its beauty.

Dazzled, he looked at his own soaring wingtips. Such glitter and color! And how pleasantly warm the heat from the ball was, now that he was closer to earth.

"What pretty feathers I have!" he bragged. "And if it weren't for me there would be no sun in the sky."

Coyote heard Hawk's loud boasts but he didn't care, because he could see too, with this wonderful new light. He looked at his poor bleeding front paws and he saw the fine shiny yellow coat that he wore. He looked at the beautiful things in the world all around him: the trees and the brooks and the golden waving grasses and the snow on the mountains high above. He knew that it had taken both a Coyote and a Hawk to bring *Da*, the Sun, into the world.

But soon Coyote became dissatisfied because Sun moved so fast that time after time it disappeared and there were dark spans called nights.

When Coyote talked to Hawk about the darkness returning whenever Sun went away, Hawk only sniffed.

"Sme-e-rk," he said to Coyote. "You wanted the world lighted and I did it. Are you never satisfied?" He went away and sunned himself on a rock.

But Coyote was smart. He knew how to manage Hawk. He made another bundle of tules and took them to the rock where Hawk was sunning himself.

"Hawk," he said, "you are a wonderful bird! You brought light to the world because you can fly so high!"

Hawk was pleased. He preened his feathers.

"Hawk, you can do something more for the world. Indians will always love you. All people will remember you, if you can do this."

"What?" asked Hawk.

"Take this bundle of tules up high, when it is night, and light them and there will never be night again."

Hawk, feeling happy to be such a fine high flying bird, took the second bunch of tules when it got dark and he soared upward.

But this time, when the spark flew up from the flints, the tules did not blaze as they had before. They burned in a pale way, with a silver smoke.

And so it is that *Alaca*, the Moon, burns with a dim and uncertain light in the night sky.

Sometimes North Wind blows "Whe-e-on" so hard that Moon is only a thin splinter of light. Sometimes Moon is only a quarter lighted and sometimes it has a bite out of it.

Coyote blamed himself for giving Hawk damp tules to make Moon.

That is why whenever the moon is full, Coyote's great grandsons and even his cousins, the dogs, sit on their haunches and howl "Ye—ouw, the moon is too dim."

Why Grizzly Bears
Walk on All Fours

Far north of where the Gabrielino Indians live, another
group of Indians have their homes at the base of a great
mountain. This mountain, called Mt. Shasta, rises so
high that its white peak pricks the sky. Indians living
around Mt. Shasta believe this mountain was made before any other mountain in the whole world.

In the long winter evenings, in the red light of the fires, their Medicine Man told them the story of how Mt. Shasta was made:

Old-Man-Above looked down from his place above the clouds and saw how flat the land was. He decided to make a high mountain for California. He took a very sharp-pointed stone in his hands and began boring a hole right down through the sky. He worked and worked until the hole was very large. Then he took bundles of snow and ice in his hands and pushed them through the hole. Down and down the snow and ice fell to the flat land below. Where it landed there was a mound. Old-Man-Above pushed more snow and more ice down through the hole in the sky. Slowly, the gleaming mound below grew larger and higher.

Old-Man-Above kept on. The mound of snow and ice grew into a small hill, the small hill grew into a big hill, and finally the big hill grew into a mountain — a mountain so high that its peak came thrusting right up into the clouds.

Then Old-Man-Above stepped down from a cloud onto the great icy pile, and from the pile onto the earth.

He wanted to make the base of Mt. Shasta pretty and green.

"Trees, grow," he ordered.

The trees sprang up, their green leaves sparkling. They grew big and tall in the wink of an eye.

Old-Man-Above turned to the yellow sun shining above the new mountain. "Sun," he said, "melt snow and turn it into water for trees to drink."

Sun made his rays stronger on the mountain's snowy

peak. Snow turned into streams of water that went tumbling down the sides of Mt. Shasta to water the trees. But there was more water than trees needed. Extra water became deep rushing rivers.

"I must make some birds to live in the trees," Old-Man-Above said to himself and picked some leaves.

With one breath he blew on the leaves and they turned into birds.

Still he was not satisfied. There should be other living and moving creatures besides the birds.

He took a stick from a tree and broke it into pieces. "Small ends, you shall be fishes to live in this beautiful running water," he cried, and threw these small ends into the water of rivers—and they turned into fishes and began to swim.

"Middle part of sticks, you shall be all kinds of animals—except the grizzly bear. The grizzly bear will be the big end of my stick."

All the sticks turned into animals. There were skinny animals and fat ones, swift animals and slow, big and little. All of these ran, hopped, jumped, or crawled on all fours. All except the grizzly bear. He reared right up on his hind legs and walked on his two hind feet like Man. He held his great, shaggy paws up in front like hands.

Old-Man-Above looked at Grizzly standing there, seeming almost as big as the new mountain, and he felt a chill of fear. Grizzly was too big! And so cunning!

"If only I hadn't made Grizzly out of such a big stick!" he said.

But it was too late. Grizzly was made.

Old-Man-Above decided to make a place for himself

where he would be safe from Grizzly. So he turned to Mt. Shasta and thought: why wouldn't that make a nice hut for when I want to live down on earth? At once he went to work digging into the mountainside. He hollowed earth out so that he had a vast room right under the mountain, with the sky shining through a round hole at the top.

Smoke was soon seen curling up into the blue sky from Mt. Shasta, where Old-Man-Above and his family lived — and still live, though their fire is alight no longer, now that the white man is in the land.

One day a terrible storm blew from the sea.

"Whang!" went Wind against the side of Old-Man-Above's hut. The mountain shook.

"Whang! Whang! WHANG!" Wind banged against the mountain until it shook the very base.

"I'm afraid!" cried Old-Man-Above's wife, "You must make *Aska*, Wind, stop before this hut falls down on us."

"I'm too tired to go all that way up to the hole where the smoke goes out," Old-Man-Above told her.

He called his beautiful little daughter, *Atche*, to him. *Atche* means Day in our language. *Atche* was small and had pretty ears like sea shells and big brown eyes and long, long black hair.

"You go up to the opening on top and tell Wind to stop shaking our hut," he told her. "But don't put your head out! Just stick out your arm and signal my message to Wind."

The little girl hurried up to the hole in the mountain's roof and did as she was told. But just as she turned to go back down Wind blew harder.

"Wham-whang!" it went against the top of the mountain until the top almost blew off.

Atche wondered why Wind hadn't stopped when she told him to stop. She wanted to see what was going on out there.

She had heard all about the rivers and trees and the ocean with waves that banged into foam on the shore, but she had never seen them. Now was her chance to take just one little look at the world. No one would ever know.

So she popped her head up over the edge, to look at the world.

"Whizz!" Wind grabbed her by her streaming long hair, pulled her out of the hole and blew her down the mountainside.

"Ge-bobble—gebobble," she went over the soft snow, with nothing to clutch at, not even a tree twig, because she was too high up for trees to grow and she was going very fast in the strong wind.

"Ca-hump—ca-hump," she rolled over rocks and down past trees toward the land where Grizzlies lived.

There was a family of Grizzlies living at the foot of Mt. Shasta. When *Atche* stopped rolling she landed right near the Grizzly family's place.

The father bear was coming home from hunting, with his club over his shoulder and a dead elk under his arm. Suddenly he saw the child of Old-Man-Above lying beneath a tree. She was stretched out on the snow with her thick black hair tangled around her.

Father Grizzly stopped and stared, then he dropped his club and the elk and rushed forward. He bent over the girl, mumbling, "What kind of creature is this?" A strange, tender warmth flared up in Grizzly's heart. He picked up the shivering little girl, and pushed her dark, tangled hair back from her face. Her skin was the lovely reddish brown of a manzanita trunk. Her hair was as glossy as a blackbird's wing. Her lips were red as the sun coming over the mountain.

"I'll take this home to my wife," Grizzly muttered. "I'll snuggle it up in my fur and keep it warm. Mother Grizzly will know what to do with it."

Gently, he tucked the girl under one huge, hairy arm, then gathered his club and his elk under the other arm and went home.

Mother Grizzly was surprised almost out of her winter coat when she saw what Father Grizzly had brought home to her. There was a slightly worried look in her deep-set eyes. Could this be Old-Man-Above's daughter, she wondered uneasily? The child was so lovely Mother Grizzly wanted to keep her, so she said only, "We'll feed the creature and keep her warm and have her for a pet."

All Grizzly's sons stood by watching while Grizzly put more wood on the fire and Mother Grizzly combed *Atche's* tangled hair and fed her.

In no time at all they all loved the strange new creature. The young girl became one of the family.

The Grizzlies never tired of looking at *Atche's* long hair and big brown eyes and her lovely red mouth. They taught her their Grizzly language. Every time she learned a new word they gave her tidbits of meat as a reward.

So the girl grew up with them and the Grizzly Nation was very proud of her. They wanted to do something

very fine for her.

One day Father Grizzly sent out a call to the whole Grizzly Nation — to the north, to the south, to the east and to the west.

"Come," he said, "come quickly and be ready to work."

"Plod, plod," came the Grizzlies, from north, south, east and west. They crunched through snow and ice. They crashed through the forests. They swam the rivers and finally arrived at Mt. Shasta.

"Now that you are here," said Grizzly, "each of you dig as hard as you can with your paws. We are going to make a fine earth hut as big as a mountain."

All the Grizzlies had a feast first, for *Atche*. Then they dug and hacked and shoveled with their paws and built a mountain hut for the girl near the one that Old-Man-Above had built. The mountain is still there and is now known as Shastina.

Many snows fell and melted and flowed into the rivers. Mother Grizzly became very old and feeble — so feeble that she could hardly walk around. It took a lot of wood to keep her warm in spite of her heavy fur coat. She thought she would soon die.

Because she was a woman bear and knew things men bears never could know, she knew that the beautiful creature she had taken in was the daughter of Old-Man-Above, and she was troubled.

She couldn't sleep nights, because she felt guilty about keeping *Atche*. And she worried about what Old-Man-Above would do when he learned the truth. Yet, she knew the time had come when Old-Man-Above must be told.

One day she called the Grizzlies together at the new hut, Shastina. Then she pulled her eldest grandson close to her.

"You must climb up and up, even through the clouds, to the top of Mt. Shasta and tell Old-Man-Above that his daughter still lives. Tell him where to find her," she told Young Grizzly. "It will be hard, but you have Grizzly strength to do anything. Just call the news down the great hole and surprise Old-Man-Above."

Young Grizzly was a fine big fellow. He had strong legs and a strong back and was sure-footed. He promised to go.

The climb was hard and he had to stop for breath often when he got up high on the mountain. His heart beat fast with fear, too. What if he couldn't get away fast enough after he had called down through the hole? What if Old-Man-Above killed him?

Finally, Grizzly courage wiped away the fear from his heart and he went on and on and up and up — until he was above the clouds of Mt. Shasta. He sat for a while and rested and looked over the ridges of mountains to the blue-green sea far beyond.

"Your child still lives!" he called in a booming voice down through the hole to Old-Man-Above inside the mountain. He waited, listening for an answer. All that he heard was the echo of his own shout rolling around the rocky hole, and the loud beat of his heart.

"Your child still *lives!*" he roared louder, with the last of his courage. "She is down the mountain on the south side." He whirled and ran back to the Grizzlies, his feet pounding on Mt. Shasta's long slope.

When Old-Man Above heard the news, he climbed out of his big hut as fast as lightning and raced down the south side of the mountain so swiftly that the snow melted along his path, as it remains to this day.

The Grizzlies prepared a great welcome for him.

As he came toward their home he saw them standing in two long files on each side of the path leading to the door of the great earth hut, Shastina. They had their clubs under their arms. The shaggy lines went as far as

Old-Man-Above could see! And there, between the two
lines of Grizzlies, stood his daughter *Atche*, full grown!

Old-Man-Above blinked, hardly believing this tall
young woman could be the little daughter who had disappeared so long ago. But he knew that she was his
daughter. As he looked at her a deep rage gathered in
his chest. He thought of all the years Grizzlies had kept
her from him — years of loneliness and sorrow.

34

With a howl of anger, Old-Man-Above turned on Mother Grizzly. He scowled, such rage glittering in his eyes, that Mother Grizzly fell back and died on the spot!

At this the bears set up a frightful howl.

Old-Man-Above swooped his daughter onto his shoulder, turned to the Grizzlies and in his fury put a curse on them.

"Peace!" he cried. "Be silent forever. Let no word ever again come from your lips — for this dreadful thing you have done by keeping my daughter from me! Never again shall you stand upright! You shall use your hands, too, for feet and always look down!"

The Grizzlies fell on all fours, their howls silenced. Their heads drooped.

Old-Man-Above drove them all away to the rivers below. He shut the door of Shastina forever and carried his daughter up Mt. Shasta.

Old-Man-Above and *Atche* have never been seen by people since that time. And since then the Grizzlies have never been able to speak. They walk on all four feet like other animals.

Indians living near Shasta look up to Grizzlies because the Grizzlies have great strength — and because once, long ago Grizzlies looked on the face of Old-Man-Above and his daughter *Atche.*

How Coyote Got His Voice

Long ago when the moon came up over Mt. Diablo, and all was quiet except for Coyote "Yeowing" from the very top of the mountain, the Medicine Man called the Yokuts Indians together. This is the story he told them about how Coyote got his voice:

Once all the world was flooded except the place where Great Eagle Chief lived. Mt. Diablo and one other tall peak were all that stuck up out of the water.

Coyote lived on top of Mt. Diablo. He was the only living thing in the world except the fleas that lived on his back.

Coyote was very lonely. He wanted company, so he sat on his haunches and tried to call out for someone else to come and stay with him on the mountain.

But Coyote had no voice. All the sound he could make was a soft whisper like "S-s-wish."

He "S-s-wished" and "S-s-wished" the whole day — except when he scratched the fleas on his back. No one came, so he went to sleep.

The second day his strained throat was sore. But loneliness in his heart ached more than his throat.

Once more he called with all his might.

That day, when the muscles in his throat stretched a little and the pain went, Coyote managed to make the whisper just a little bit louder.

But only the swishing water heard him as it slapped against the top of Mt. Diablo. Water mimicked Coyote by saying, "We-osh, we-osh."

Coyote grew very tired. His throat was dry from we-oshing all day. He took a drink of water, then scratched the fleas down near his tail and went to sleep again.

The third day, loneliness was still in his heart like a heavy stone. Once more he started we-oshing, over and over and over in the hope that someone would hear him.

Suddenly that very low whispered we-osh sound got a tiny bit louder way down in his throat. It went "Wow-osh." No one heard Coyote but Water and Wind. Together they worked to imitate him. Wind blew harder and Water "we-oshed" a little more until it sounded exactly like Coyote's loud "Wow-osh."

There was nothing for Coyote to do but take a drink of water, scratch a few fleas, then go to sleep and wait for another day.

On the fourth day, Coyote wow-oshed again and again. He was so lonely that his heart swelled with loneliness and he could hardly wow-osh at all.

Water and Wind kept making fun of him by wow-oshing just the way he did!

Just before night came over the mountain, that wow-osh of Coyote's grew a little louder. It gave poor Coyote courage to keep on trying. He scratched his fleas and settled down to sleep once more.

On the fifth day, early in the morning, when dawn was very pink, Coyote woke up. He shook himself and made the fleas scurry around his tail. He combed his whiskers with his paws, took a drink of water and went to work.

"Surely," he thought, "if I keep trying someone will hear me and come."

"Wow-osh," he started with his tight throat—"Wow-osh—come and see me."

All morning he did this, panting when he paused to catch his breath.

About noon, when the sun was directly over his head, that "Wow-osh" grew quite loud. It was loud enough to go a long way across the water. Coyote danced for joy all alone on the mountain top and called in his new, loud voice until he was hoarse.

His call was even louder than all the noise Wind and Water tried to make. That made Coyote feel pretty fine, even though his throat was sore and nobody replied.

He was so tired that night when he lay down to sleep that he didn't even bother to scratch at his fleas.

"Let those fleas chase," he thought. "I don't care — the silly things."

On the sixth day, Coyote was late starting with his wow-oshing. The sun was high in the sky and the water was washing hard around the base of Mt. Diablo.

Coyote took his time getting ready that morning, because he felt that this would be a special day. First, he scratched at his fleas until they ran from the back of his ears to his shoulders. Then he made them scamper across his stomach and race down to his tail.

"That will tire them and make them be quiet for a while," he told himself.

After the flea chase he washed his face with his paws, combed his whiskers carefully and took time to shake out his bushy yellow tail. He settled down on his haunches, ready to start wailing with the hope that someone, some-where, would come. He opened his jaws wide and let the sound come. The howl that rushed past his long white teeth was the loudest he had ever made. It was so loud and long that for a moment Coyote just sat there blink-ing in surprise and joy. Then he opened his mouth and let the call pour out again and again.

"Ye--owe! Ye---owe!" went across the water. He thought that even Mt. Diablo shook a little when he called!

"That should bring company to me," he thought.

When he was quiet for a time to catch his breath, he

suddenly heard the great Eagle God whisper in his big yellow ear.

"Well done, Coyote. I wondered if you would keep at it until you got your voice. Today your 'Ye-owe' was loud enough for me to hear way up here. Keep on calling for company, and watch. I have a surprise for you—a reward for your patience and courage."

Coyote kept on "Ye-owing." He watched the water and the peak of the other mountain far away.

Then, when the day grew hot and he was tired and nothing had happened, Coyote wondered if the whisper from Eagle could have been just his own thoughts. But he kept on watching.

Suddenly, right before his eyes there was a single feather bobbing around on the water. As Coyote watched, flesh and bones came — more feathers. They joined themselves to the first little feather and turned into a beautiful eagle!

There was a stir on the water, a rush of broad wings and before the widening ripples reached the mountain top, a beautiful bird with tawny gold breast feathers and lovely brown back feathers and sharp brown eyes stood beside surprised Coyote.

Coyote nearly shook out of his yellow skin with joy at having such a beautiful bird beside him for company on Mt. Diablo.

"Your feathers are so shiny," he said, and rubbed Eagle's back with his long yellow nose in a caress. "You are so beautiful I just want to look and look and look at you."

"And I like to look at you," Eagle said. "Your own fur

40

is a beautiful yellow, Coyote. It is the golden yellow of Sun. And your tail! Well, that tail of yours is the most beautiful thing I have ever seen!" Then Eagle stroked Coyote's back with his great beak.

Coyote, being cunning to get his own way, said: "Would you mind looking for the flea up by my ear where I can't reach? That flea is the cleverest of the lot. I never can catch him."

Eagle caught Coyote's flea and dropped it into the water below.

That made Coyote happy. He thanked Eagle.

Eagle liked Coyote's voice and told him so. "All I can do is screech — a very harsh loud screech. But I do like to hear you sing."

Coyote sang and sang for Eagle. When he had finished, he and Eagle settled down for a long talk. They talked for hours and hours. They talked for days. Coyote told how hard it had been for him to learn to sing, and of how long he had worked in order to call loudly enough for anyone to hear him. Near the end of the story, Coyote saw Eagle look off toward the other peak that stuck up out of the water!

Coyote's heart began to beat very fast. He was afraid Eagle would fly away and leave him.

Coyote kept his fears to himself and began "Ye-owe--oweing" as sweetly as he could.

Finally, one day, Eagle grew restless. He stretched his wings. He stood on his tip-claws and looked hard over at the mountain peak beyond.

Then he said: "Coyote, I'm tired of catching your fleas and listening to your songs. Let's go over to that other peak and see what is there."

"No — I can't," Coyote sighed. His heart turned over so hard in sadness that he hoped Eagle didn't see it bumping under his yellow fur. "You can fly there, Eagle, but I'm only a coyote with four legs. I can't fly."

"Nonsense, where's your courage?" Eagle asked. "Once you couldn't sing—remember? Now look how beautifully you can 'Ye-owe-owe.' Just try to swim. I'll fly slowly and hover over the water above you. I'll pull you out with my great claws if you start to sink."

Still Coyote held back, afraid. He looked at the water so deep and blue around the peak and shivered.

"Surely you have as much courage as an eagle who cannot sing!" Eagle prodded.

Coyote still hung back. There was nothing for his feet to stand on once he got into that cold water. "No — no I can't."

"Very well," said Eagle, "I'm going. Either try to swim and I'll help you — or stay here alone."

That was enough for Coyote. He had known great loneliness and he loved Eagle. He couldn't bear to be parted from his beautiful friend.

Without a backward look he plunged into the water and worked his legs as fast as he could. He didn't sink. He found he could swim very fast without getting out of breath.

"What did I tell you?" Eagle "shrooked" from above him. "All you needed was courage, Coyote."

They went across the water fast. Eagle kept sharp watch over Coyote, to be sure he was safe.

The fleas on Coyote hated the water. They ran from

his legs. They ran from his sides. They ran from the thin fur on his stomach up to the middle of his back. Then a great wave came that covered his back and the fleas were all washed away!

Finally, Eagle and Coyote reached the distant peak.

When Eagle had smoothed down his wind-blown feathers, and Coyote had shaken all the water off his fur, Eagle patted Coyote with his great beak.

"I wasn't going to leave you back on that mountain at all," he said. "I just wanted you to try something new — and get rid of those fleas."

Then they both laughed.

Eagle and Coyote stayed many days on the new peak. Then they began to be lonely for other creatures. There were no other creatures. There were no more peaks to swim or fly to.

"Let's *do* something about being lonely," Coyote said to Eagle. "Surely, you with your fine courage and feathers and sharp eyes, and I with my yellow coat and strong legs and good voice, can think up something very good."

They thought hard. Coyote was willing to share his voice and his ability to run fast and swim. Eagle was willing to share his sharp eyes, his great courage and his ability to fly.

So they created the Yokuts Indian men and Yokuts Indian women of Mt. Diablo. These Indians multiplied and brought Indian girls and Indian boys into the world.

The peak grew very crowded. Great Eagle saw that more room was needed. He told Water to go down from Water's high place near the top of the mountain. Water slid back and back until where it had been there were

only trees and grass and dry land—just as it is around
Mt. Diablo today.

The Medicine Man told his people this story over and
over for they never grew tired of hearing how they got
their courage and sharp eyes from Eagle, and their fine
voices, swift feet, and swimming ability from Coyote.

How Animals Brought Fire to Man

On cold nights when all the Karoks along the Klamath River were warm around the fire, the story-teller waved his story-telling staff and told how Karoks got their fire.

In the beginning, Fire was given to two old hags, because they were the very oldest people on earth. These hags were to share *Oh*, the Fire, with the Indians. Instead, the old hags kept Fire for themselves.

The Karoks shivered with the cold. They needed Fire to warm their hands and backs on cold nights. They wanted their children to see the pretty yellow flames dance. So they tried in every way they could think of to get Fire away from the two greedy old hags.

The old women were fearsome creatures. One had four teeth. She gnashed her teeth together and they rattled like stones.

The other had five teeth in her flabby old mouth. The sound she made was far worse than stones rattling.

The hags had stringy hair, tied in a knot on top of their heads with a string of nettles. They were so thin their bones clattered when they walked.

The old hags rattled and growled every time an Indian came near the hut where they lived. They chased Indians with clubs in their bony hands. They threatened to claw Indian eyes out with their fingers that had nails on them like claws of Eagle.

One winter night when it was colder than it had ever been before, the Karoks were desperate. Shivering, they went to Coyote and told him their troubles.

"Unless we get Fire we will be so cold we will shake our bones apart, then the bones will rattle out of our skins and we will be dead," they told Coyote. "You are crafty and clever and cunning. Please steal Fire away from those hags for us."

Coyote felt very sorry for the Indians, because he was warm in his yellow coat of fur and they had no snug fur coats to keep them warm. He thought of taking off his coat and giving it to them, but it didn't have any openings through which he could get out.

He rubbed his whiskers and thought and thought. But no idea for a way of stealing Fire came to him.

Then he shook his tail hard, so hard that the earth around him shook too. Only, shaking his tail didn't shake a thought into his head about how to steal Fire from the old hags.

His fleas bothered him. If he could just get rid of those

miserable fleas, he mused, maybe he could think better. He rolled on the ground, stirring up clouds of dust. The dust blinded the fleas and choked them. They stopped biting Coyote while they sneezed and coughed and tried to wipe the dust from their eyes.

While the fleas were wiping themselves off, an idea came to Coyote.

He called the Indians and animals together and told them he had a plan for stealing Fire.

Then, from the land of Karoks to the house of the old

hags, he stationed a great company of animals, each animal at a distance from the other. The strongest animal was placed nearest to the den of the hags. The weakest animal was the farthest away. Last of all, Coyote hid a Karok Indian to wait near the hags' hut.

Coyote told the Karok exactly what to do, then trotted up the mountain to the door of the old hags.

Coyote knocked softly, politely, on the door.

The hags didn't hear him. They were fighting, and rattling their teeth at each other.

Coyote knocked again, more loudly.

The door opened and the hag with four teeth stuck her head out.

"What do you want?" she asked through her teeth.

"Would you please let me in out of the cold?" Coyote asked politely. He shivered a little to show her how cold he was, though he really was very warm with excitement.

The old hag suspected nothing. After all, he was polite. She had no grudge against Coyote, except that he "Ye— owed" too loud and too long on moonlight nights and kept her awake.

"All right, come in," she grumbled. "But for my poor ear's sake don't start 'ye—owe—owing' tonight."

Coyote had learned a long time ago when to sing and when to be quiet. This certainly was the time to be quiet. Everything depended on his manners.

He tip-pawed as softly as he knew how on every one of his four paws, to the hearth. He lay down before the crackling fire and made himself comfortable. Now all he needed was to wait for the Karok hiding in the woods to do his part.

Coyote's ears perked up. He heard the Karok coming along the trail.

Suddenly the Indian made a furious attack on the hut. Crash! Bang! His club thudded against the place, rattling the walls.

The old hags rushed out, gnashing their teeth.

That was Coyote's chance! He seized a half-burned brand in his mouth and fled from the hut like a comet, and down the mountain.

The two hags had sharp ears and eyes. They saw Coyote and took after him.

Coyote ran as fast as he could. But he had eaten more than the hags and was fatter.

They were so thin they had only bones to carry and they could run very, very, *very* fast.

Coyote's breath was giving out! The hags were so close he could feel their breath blowing on his tail. He could hear their teeth rattling.

Gasping, Coyote looked around for help. He couldn't run any more. Just as one old hag grabbed at his tail, something leaped from the bushes. Mountain Lion! Mountain Lion seized the flaming brand between his white teeth and raced on.

Coyote sank down, clearing his sooty eyes and throat and catching his breath. Through the roaring in his own ears, he heard the old hags scream in anger and gnash their teeth more wildly than ever as they rushed by him and after Mountain Lion.

Mountain Lion went so fast that he left a trail of sparks in the cold damp night.

Even Mountain Lion could not out-race the fleet hags.

50

They were about to catch him by the tail when Bear jumped out of a cave! Bear grabbed the torch in his great claws and took off with it.

But Bear couldn't go as fast as Mountain Lion, because he had robbed too many bees of their honey that year and he was big and fat.

"Kerthunk — wobble," he waddled. Bear got winded very soon. The old hags soon caught up with him. They had only knots of hair and bones to weigh them down and they didn't have as heavy teeth as Bear had.

Bear was so near to being caught that he had to throw the torch toward the place where Rabbit was supposed to be hiding.

"What if Rabbit isn't there?" Bear thought. "What if Rabbit doesn't catch the brand and the hags get Fire back?" Bear was sorry he had eaten so much honey and was so fat. If Indians lost Fire they would blame him and the honey inside his fat belly.

But Rabbit was there in his place by the bush. He caught up the torch and didn't mind a bit that his whiskers were singed.

"Hoppity-hoppity-hop" he went, right from under the

bony, reaching fingers of the old hags, and down the mountain path as hard as he could hop.

On went the torch from one animal to the next with the old hags after it.

Poor Squirrel, the next to the last animal on the trail to the Indian village, burned his tail so badly that it curled up over his back — where it remains to this day.

Last came Frog, who didn't get the brand until it had burned down to a very little piece. He hopped along so heavily that the old hags gained on him.

They kept coming nearer and nearer and NEARER and faster and faster and F-A-S-T-E-R!

Frog pulled his back legs up very tight and made a great spring.

Still the hags gained on him.

They were about up to him. He could feel their breath on the back of his neck! He stretched himself at each leap until his poor muscles went "crackety crack."

Then he was caught! His smoke-dried eyes bulged out of his head. His little heart thumped like a club against the cold bony fingers that closed over his body.

He made a wild "Croak!" the first croak he had ever made in all his life. "I'll make one more hop for the Karoks! One more hop for Coyote who trusted me in this great thing!" he vowed.

With a mighty gulp, brave little Frog swallowed Fire, tore himself away from the bony old hands that held him, and leaped into the river.

He dived deep and swam furiously until he reached the other side of the river where the hags could not follow. There he sank down, gasping with his last breath.

But alas, he had left his beautiful tail in the hands of one old hag. Worse, there was only his ghost left to spit out a burning ember onto some sticks.

It is because Frog's ghost coughed out that ember that Indians can make Fire by rubbing two sticks of wood together. And it is because Frog lost his tail that, ever since, only the young Frogs called tadpoles have tails.

Although Coyote ran until his paws were raw — and Rabbit singed his whiskers — and Squirrel scorched his tail so that it curled up over his back — and Frog lost his tail forever — not one of the animals has ever spoken of the sacrifices made in bringing Fire to the Indians by the Klamath River.

What Happened to Six Wives
Who Ate Onions

Western Mono Indians lived high up on the Kings River. They knew how to use magic.

Here is a story they told:

Once there were six pretty Mono wives. These wives had six husbands who were mountain lion hunters.

One day, while the husbands were out hunting, the wives went up the mountain to pick clover for food. That day, one wife discovered something new to eat — wild onions.

"Yum, these new plants taste better than anything I've ever eaten!" she told the others. "Just taste this."

The other wives all tasted the onions. They liked them too. They ate and ate and smacked their lips and then went home to cook supper for their husbands.

Just as dusk was falling the husbands came plodding

home. Each had killed a big mountain lion.

"Phew! What's that odor?" the husbands asked their wives when they got to the hut door. They came closer to their wives and discovered the terrible odor was on the breath of their wives!

"We found this new plant to eat—just taste it," the wives said and offered some to the husbands.

"No!" they cried in disgust. "Your breath is enough for us—horrible!" They wouldn't even taste the onions.

That night the husbands made their wives stay outdoors because the odor of onions kept them awake.

It was cold outside and the wives didn't like to stay out there alone without their husbands.

The next day when the husbands had gone hunting, the wives went back to where the onions grew and ate more than they had the day before. Those onions were so tasty, they just couldn't help eating them.

When the husbands came home for supper, not one of them had slain a mountain lion. Never before had they come home without mountain lions and they were very sad.

"Mountain lions smelled that horrible odor on us," they grumbled. "Mountain lions ran away fast before we could get near enough to catch them."

The wives didn't believe their husbands and said so.

But when the husbands smelled the odor of onions stronger than ever, they scolded.

"You can't come near us! You are worse than skunks."

Again, they wouldn't let their wives come inside the hut to sleep. They wouldn't put food out for their wives to eat.

The wives went home to their fathers and mothers, but that didn't do any good. They were sent right back to their husbands.

This lasted six days. Each night the men came home without mountain lions and each night they found their wives had been eating onions again.

Finally, what with the strong odor of onions and not getting mountain lions, the husbands went into a terrible rage.

"Go away!" they shouted. "Go away! We can't hunt! We can't sleep nights because you eat so many onions. We don't want you any more. Go away!"

The next morning when the husbands had gone, the wives all went up the mountain to where onions grew. Each of them took her magic rope made of eagle's down.

They were hungry and missed the mush and they were tired of sleeping alone in the cold outside the hut at night.

"Let's leave our husbands forever," one wife said. "Our husbands don't like us any more."

They all agreed.

So they climbed and climbed up a big rock. Each wife carried her eagle-down rope. One wife brought her little girl with her.

At last, they reached the very top of the rock. They rested awhile, then the leader of the wives said, "Now is the time for magic. Do you still want to leave your husbands forever?"

"Yes!" they all cried.

So the leader of the wives said a magic Mono word and threw her eagle-down rope up into the sky.

"Whosh!" it went, straight up. The center of the rope caught on a piece of the sky so that both ends of the rope hung down to the rock.

The women tied all their own ropes to the ends of the rope hanging from the sky. Then they clasped hands and called:

"Eagle-down ropes, magic ropes, help us!"

They stood on the ropes which were spread on the rock and began to sing to the magic ropes, with a special magic song.

Then, because they knew so much magic and had magic ropes, the ropes slowly began to rise and swing around and around the way Buzzard flies.

As the wives sang louder the ropes made bigger and bigger circles in the sky.

Soon the women standing on the ropes were sailing through the sky over the village where they lived.

Their fathers and mothers looked up and saw them in the sky. People of the village pointed up at them and were very excited.

The women in the sky saw their mothers and fathers and their mothers-in-law and fathers-in-law rush into huts. Next they saw them come out with mush and beads and belts and put all these things on the ground.

"Come back!" the women's relatives cried up at them. "Come back and see what we have for you!"

But the women just stayed in the sky.

Down below, the husbands looked up and saw their wives. "Why didn't you keep an eye on them?" they scolded their wives' parents. "Why did you let them get away when we were out hunting?"

Now that the wives were gone, the husbands wanted them back. They were lonesome and sad. They got together and tried to think what to do.

They decided to use their own magic eagle-down ropes and go up in the sky after their wives.

They climbed the rock, put down their ropes and sang in the same way their wives had done. Soon they were sailing in the sky over the village.

Old people came out and begged their sons to come back, but the sons wanted their wives, so they kept on singing and going higher and higher into the sky.

By this time the wives were very high in the sky because they had a head start on the husbands. They looked down and saw their husbands coming after them.

"Shall we let them catch us?" they asked each other.

"No!" said one. "Our husbands said they didn't want us any more. Don't let them catch up with us, ever."

All agreed they would rather be alone in the sky.

As soon as the husbands got close enough, the women shouted down. "Stay where you are!"

The wives had stronger magic in their eagle-down ropes and their magic song. The men had to stay right where they were — below their wives.

They all turned into stars where they are to this day.

White men call the higher group of six stars the Pleiades. Indians call them the Young Women. The lower set of six stars, white men call Taurus. Indians call them the Young Men.

Whatever the name, there they are, swinging slowly across the sky on clear nights — and all because the Mono Indian women loved to eat wild onions more than anything else.

How the First Rainbow Was Made

Long ago, when Indians were the only people in California, the story-teller of the Achomawi Indians living along the Pit River told this story:

Many moons ago there was a very wet winter and Indians had no way of finding out when the sky would clear. So much rain came down that they couldn't go hunting and they couldn't gather seeds to eat. They grew hungrier day by day.

They put on their blue-jay feather headdresses and their feather capes and looked up into the sky while they sang and danced their best dances for Old-Man-Above. But Old-Man-Above kept sending down rain.

For three moons they sang and danced and still no

answer came from Old-Man-Above. Then Chief Flicker-Feathers had an idea.

"Let's go ask Coyote what to do. Coyote has been on earth longer than Indians and he is very wise."

They slosh—sloshed in single file through the rain in a long parade to the cave where Coyote lived.

Coyote met them at the mouth of his dry cave. He was glad to see them, because staying alone there to keep out of the rain was very tiresome.

When the visitors had taken off their wet feather headdresses and capes and were settled, Chief Flicker-Feathers told Coyote about the trouble and asked him what to do.

Coyote scratched his fleas a bit, then said, "You go away and let me think for a while. I will ask Old-Man-Above what to do."

So the Indians went back through the rain to their huts to wait.

Coyote thought for a while, then tried high singing yelps in an effort to reach Old-Man-Above.

"Ye—owe-ow," he sang and sang as sweetly as he knew how.

But Old-Man-Above didn't pay any attention. He was too busy pushing the clouds around into newer and prettier patterns in the sky.

Coyote shook out his tail, and took a drink of water to ease his throat after all the singing. Next, he trotted around the woods for a while to see if any ideas would jiggle into his furry yellow head.

He clattered and scrambled over stones and logs and over rough trails. Suddenly, he saw Spider Woman swing down on her rope from the top of the tallest tree in the forest. A plan sprang into his mind.

He brushed up his whiskers and shook himself three times so his damp fur would fluff out. Then he went to the bush where Spider Woman and her sixty sons lived in the center of a big spider web.

Coyote told her his plan and asked her to help him.

She only wobbled her shiny black body from side to side. "I'm too old to work so hard," she said. "I'm too fat and heavy for the job."

Coyote drooped his ears and looked so sad, she felt sorry for him.

"I'll lend you two of my youngest sons. They will be light as thistle down and they can make spider rope faster than any of my other sons."

She called her two youngest sons.

"Whizz!" Each came running on his eight legs as fast as he could. They were fine black shiny fellows eager for adventure. Coyote told them his plan.

"Good!" they cried. "We'll help you!" They began exercising up and down on their black legs to show what strong fellows they were, then they got their rope baskets and set off along the trail in the rain with Coyote.

They hadn't gone far when they met the two White-Footed Mice Boys sker-mo-rooting around in the bushes for seeds and greens to eat.

Coyote told them his plans. "Will you boys help?"

"Yes," said one as he poked greens into his mouth.

They all walked along the trail together up Mt. Shasta until they met Weasel Man, who had just poked his head out of a hole to see what kind of a day it was.

Coyote told his plan to Weasel Man. "Will you help?"

"Of course," said Weasel Man as he stretched his long slender body and gave his tail a flick, before he joined them on the trail up Mt. Shasta.

Before long they came onto Red Fox Woman swishing her big yellow tail around in the bushes, hunting for her supper. Her eyes grew very big and excited when Coyote told her his plan.

"I want to come too," she said, and fell in line.

Just then, Rabbit Woman poked her head around a bush. She wanted to go too if Fox Woman was going.

All the animals went long the trail together until they reached the very top of Mt. Shasta. The drizzle had stopped, but the sky was still heavily clouded.

On the top of Mt. Shasta, Coyote and his animal people met the Indians who were anxious to know his plan.

Coyote smiled, wiggled his whiskers and winked at the two youngest sons of Spider Woman, then he faced the Indians.

"Now," he said, "I want the two best arrow shooters!"

The two very best shots came forward.

"Everyone come close," Coyote ordered. "Listen carefully. If anyone fails to work with all his heart and all his strength, the whole plan will fail."

He wiped his whiskers and looked very wise and then went on, "Old-Man-Above won't listen to us here on earth. He is too busy up there playing with the clouds. What we have to do is to get up there where he lives and make him listen." He pointed to the Indians.

"You two must first shoot arrows up there at exactly the same spot and make a hole in the sky."

Coyote then whirled around to the Spider Brothers who were exercising up and down on their legs. "Spider Brothers will start to work on their ropes. Weasel Man, the White-Footed Mice Boys, Fox Woman, Rabbit Woman and myself will then blow very hard."

"I don't see what good our blowing will do," Fox Woman sniffed.

"Stop talking and listen," Coyote scolded. He went on telling the plan.

"Spider Brothers will make their ropes longer as we blow both of them up through the arrow hole in the sky. Then Spider Brothers can ask Old-Man-Above what he is going to do about a sign to tell when the rain is over."

Coyote looked around at each animal in the circle and at the Indians and said. "No one has ever gone through the sky to where Old-Man-Above lives. If even one of us fails to blow hard there might not be enough breath to carry Spider Brothers up there. They will fall down and be smashed as flat as a rush mat. Are you ready?"

They all said they were ready. Each animal practiced blowing his breath, hiffing and huffing and puffing. Weasel Man put back his ears and looked skyward and went "Snoo" as hard as he could.

"Don't blow through your *nose!*" Coyote yelped at him.

Weasel Man tried again, using his mouth to blow a big "Phoo!"

Coyote then sat on his haunches and braced his front legs on the earth. "Now, when I say 'One,' get ready. When I say 'Two,' draw in your breath and you Indians get your bows ready to shoot. When I say 'Three,' Indians shoot and animals blow and no one is to stop until I say stop."

"One!" cried Coyote.

Everyone got ready. Spider Brothers stiffened their legs ready to spring.

"Two!"

The animals drew in their breath so their cheeks puffed out. The Indians raised their drawn bows.

"Three!" Coyote yelped.

"Whi-rr Whizzz" went two arrows straight up and out of sight. Where they disappeared, they left a hole in the sky.

"Whooff!" went the White-Footed Mice boys.

"Whiff!" went Red Fox Woman.

"Phuff!" went Rabbit Woman.

"Phoo!" went Weasel Man.

"Whee-whee!" went Coyote, while the Indians waited

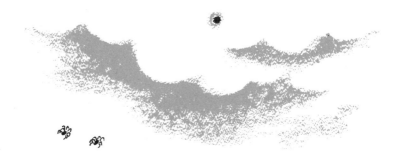

with their cheeks puffed out ready to help when the animals' breath ran out.

Up went Spider Brothers on their ropes. They had to work hard weaving rope to keep up with all the whoofs and whiffs and phuffs and phoos and whees. Their black legs went so fast, they were just a blur against the sky.

When the animal people were out of breath, the Indians blew hard until the animals were ready again. Up and up the Spider Brothers went.

Twelve times, the animals whoffed and whiffed and phuffed and phoo-wheed, and the Indians blew too.

The two Spiders were almost to the hole.

Then one Spider Brother reached up with three of his eight legs and grabbed the edge of the hole. He pulled himself up. But the other Brother couldn't make it.

"Blow—blow *harder!*" Coyote howled.

Up in the sky, the one Spider Brother was frightened. "I can't do it!" he exclaimed shrilly. "I've run out of rope!" And he began bobbling around.

"Wait until I brace three of my legs on this cloud!" his brother shouted out against the wind. He braced himself and his brother leaped. He managed to catch his brother by three legs.

The watchers below saw the Spider Brothers disappear through the hole in the sky and gave a great sigh of relief.

"We can rest now, thank goodness," panted Coyote. "Spider Brothers won't have any trouble coming down. They are used to swinging down from trees."

All sat down to wait. Waiting was hard for they didn't know how Spider Brothers were making out.

Spider Brothers were all worn out after they got up through the hole in the sky. They were sitting resting when Old-Man-Above spied them.

"What are you two black specks doing up here?" he roared as he came striding over the clouds.

He looked so very big and so very cross that the Spider Brothers were scared and all the knees of all their legs shook. They bent low in a bow on all eight of their shaky legs, then said:

"We wish to ask you if you won't please make some kind of a sign to send to earth and let folks know when the skies will clear and the rain stop falling."

With all this politeness, Old-Man-Above forgot his anger. He looked kindly at Spider Brothers and rubbed his whiskers which were made from white clouds.

"But how in the world did you get up here to tell me?" he wanted to know.

Spider Brothers told him how Coyote had thought up the plan and how everybody had helped and how hard they had worked.

"That's fine! That's wonderful!" Old-Man-Above cried joyfully. "I like everybody to work together and each to help the other." He was silent for a minute. "I can't un-

derstand," said he, "why I didn't hear the Indians or Coyote sending messages up here." Then he remembered that he was busy moving stars around and brightening them up a bit for Spring. Stars were heavy and made much noise when they were pushed around.

He invited Spider Brothers to have a basketful of mush with him. The mush was made from snowflakes with melted moonlight poured over them. Old-Man-Above said while they were eating he would think about how to make a sign that meant the rain would stop — so all on earth could see it and know.

After they all had snowflake mush together and he was comfortable lying against a white cloud, Old-Man-Above told the Spider Brothers how he planned to make the big rain-clear sign.

"You'll have to help me," said he. "Think hard about a giant fox tail. A tail big enough to stretch clear across the sky."

Spider Brothers thought hard about the big tail — like Red Fox Woman wore.

"Now think of the color of the blue-bird's back," Old-

Man-Above told them. "Think hard, so you can see that blue stripe all along the giant fox tail."

They thought hard and right before their eyes there was the stripe!

"Now, quick! Think about the red of sunrise. Hurry! A red stripe must come before the blue fades!"

So they did and there came a red streak right next to the blue — with a little overlap that made a purple stripe.

"Now, be sharp!" said Old-Man-Above. "Think of the yellow of Coyote's fur coat and put it above the red!"

They did as they were told. There came a yellow stripe like gold. Where it overlapped there was an orange stripe.

"Now think of the green when grass is just coming up! Put it there by the blue."

They thought fast and where the light green overlapped there was a dark green stripe.

"Now, for good measure, I'll take a bit of cloud and spread white by the yellow stripe and that white ought to finish off the rain-clear sign we have made together."

It took him some time to arrange the white.

The giant fox tail was so beautiful and so filled with light that its brightness hurt the Spider Brothers' eyes when they looked at it.

Then Old-Man-Above told them how the rain-clear sign was to be worked. He was going to poke his finger four times and make four holes in the sky. One hole was to be in the east, one in the west, one in the north and one in the south.

"You Spiders will make a rope at each hole, swing down to earth and fasten each rope to a bush or tree. Then climb up here on the rope again — without telling anybody. This will make four invisible posts to hold up the rain-clear sign in the sky. When I am going to clear away rain with the sun, I'll swing the giant colored fox tail around where the sign needs to be. The ends will rest on two of the posts. Now, do you Spider Brothers understand what you are to do?" They nodded.

"Well, hurry and do your work and come back to me. I'll keep the fox tail lighted until you come back."

Spider Brothers hurried away and did as they were told. They made posts that are invisible to this day. Few people except the Achomawi Indians know how the rainbow is held up.

Meanwhile, down on earth things were not going well. Making posts took so many moons that the animals grew tired of waiting below the hole in the sky. They wondered if Old-Man-Above had eaten Spider Brothers and forgotten about the rain-clear sign.

Spider Woman missed her two youngest sons. Each moon she was more lonely for them. She blamed Coyote for taking them away and blowing them up through that terrible hole. The other animals also turned on Coyote.

Poor Coyote was very sad. He went into his cave alone and howled "Ye—owe-owe" over and over because he was so sad and lonely. All the other animals had left and gone to their dens.

"I did the very best I could to help everybody," he told himself. "Now, they are blaming me for everything bad."

But the Indians felt very sorry for him. They didn't blame him because so much time had passed since Spider Brothers had gone up through the hole in the sky. They were sure that Coyote, being wise as he was, would get some good results from all his thought and everybody's work. That comforted Coyote some, but he was still sad.

All this time Spider Brothers were working hard. Finally the work was finished and the four posts made. When they went to Old-Man-Above they ached all over from going down to earth and climbing back so many times.

"You are good. You have been faithful," Old-Man-Above told them as he pushed and pulled the giant fox tail around into place.

"You did what I told you and kept it a secret — one of the hardest things to do. Now swing yourselves back to earth from that hole where you came up. When you get to earth look up into the sky and see your beautiful work. I'll have it in place then."

He patted them ever so gently on their shiny black bodies. "To reward you for all your hard work, I will give you tiny rain-clear signs of your own. When you go out mornings and dew is on your webs, wait until the sun shines. You will see your own little rainbows."

Then he shook his finger at them. "Now mind, you are not to go shooting holes through my sky and come up here to bother me any more. I'm going to plug up that hole the Indians made, with a cloud. I'll do it the minute you go through that hole back to earth."

Spider Brothers swung on their ropes back to earth and ran to their mother as fast as they could go.

Spider Woman was delighted to see her long lost sons. All fifty-eight brothers were excited, too.

The two Spider Brothers said, "We must go tell all the other animals who helped, and the Indians, too. Then, all together we will look up to see the beautiful rain-clear

sign in the sky."

Away they ran to spread the news.

All the animals came close in a great circle to hear Spider Brothers tell of their great adventure. Then, after they had finished telling the story, the brothers cried:

"Look up! See the surprise!"

Everybody looked up. The clouds parted, and there, reaching clear across the sky, was the first beautiful rainbow ever seen on earth.

The animals gave a great feast to Coyote and the brave, faithful Spider Brothers. Coyote forgot how cross everyone had been to him and how they had blamed him for all their bad luck. He was the merriest guest at the feast.

Ever since then, Spiders have had their own private rainbows. When it rains, or dew clings to their webs, there the small rainbows are, glittering in the sunlight.

How Coyote Became
a Friend to Man

The Karok Indians live along the Upper Klamath River in the very northern part of California. They love Coyote, and they have reason to love him, for Coyote is their friend.

After the rains have gone, when fresh green grass is pricking up like green arrows pointing to the sky, the Karok story-teller brings his people a treat.

First he puts on his best fur-and-feather cape. Then he gets out his story-telling staff and calls the Indians to come out and listen. He sometimes tells them this tale about how Coyote became a good friend to the Karoks.

Chareya, the maker of all things, first made fishes to use the water, then he made animals to use the land and birds to use the air. Last of all he made a man—a Karok.

Chareya gave this Karok the power to rule over all the animals and to tell each animal its duties and position in the world.

The Karok man thought and worried about the great power that *Chareya* had intrusted to him. He wondered how he could decide which animal should be chosen to be the swiftest runner, or which should be the strongest, and which should be the most cunning.

"And which of all animals shall sing the loudest?" he asked himself, and scratched his head, trying to decide.

"Who is to have the most beautiful fur?" he wondered. That was a hard choice. He wanted to be fair to all.

After many moons he got an idea.

He called all the animals — the bears, the mice, the mountain lions, the rabbits, scampering chipmunks, and the bristly porcupine. At the sound of the Karok's voice, the animals came leaping and crawling and hopping through the woods.

"Sit around me," the Karok ordered. "And listen well!"

The animals scurried into their places in a huge circle. There they sat, waiting breathlessly for what Man, their ruler, had to say.

"Tomorrow, early in the morning," the Karok began, his black eyes fixed upon the animals, "I want every one of you to be here at this spot. I am going to give a bow with arrows to each of you. The animal to whom I give the longest bow will be the highest ranking animal of all. The one to whom I give the smallest bow will be the lowest in rank."

The animals looked at each other nervously.

"Now remember," the Karok said, "be here early."

Coyote, who was sitting in the front row, twitched his tail in excitement. He pictured himself getting the biggest bow of all. He would be the highest of all the animals. Only—there was no way to be sure that the Karok would choose him.

Coyote trotted back to his den, wondering how he could manage things so that he would get the longest bow.

The Karok had said to arrive at the place early. Coyote wrinkled his brow in thought. What if he got there earlier than anyone else? Perhaps, then, the Karok would give the biggest bow to him.

"Yes!" Coyote exclaimed. "That's what I will do. In fact, I won't even sleep. I'll stay awake all night and then race to meet the Karok."

Instead of curling up in his den as he usually did, Coyote began to pace in circles in order to keep himself awake. Every time he caught himself yawning, he made himself pace a little faster.

But the rapid pacing made him very weary and the yawns started coming faster and faster. His eyelids grew so heavy that at moments he found himself running around with his eyes shut.

Coyote stopped and sat down and shook himself. His eyelids drooped, so he shook himself again, harder than before. He shook so fiercely that his bones rattled. He tried to shake sleep from his yes.

His eyes closed for an instant and he grew alarmed. He had almost fallen asleep that time! Somehow, he had to try to find a way to stay awake until it was time to go and get the great bow which he was sure the Karok would give him.

There was a stream of water near Coyote's den, so he ran, yawning and shaking himself, and plunged in. The water was cold and dark. Coyote hated the feel of Water against his skin and fur. Just the same, Water was a help. Its wetness stung his eyes. Its coldness made him shiver. He felt certain that now he would not go to sleep.

No sooner had he got back to his den than he got sleepy again. Desperately, he started singing songs to himself, songs about the giant bow and what he would do with it.

And then — just before dawn — his eyelids slipped down and down. His head drooped. His knees buckled. Coyote slid down in a snoring heap, sound asleep.

He woke up much later, with a start. His heart sank as he realized what had happened.

Coyote raced from his den. He ran faster than he had ever run. He ran into the meeting, breathless, — the last animal there!

All that was left for poor Coyote was the very shortest bow of all.

Coyote was so disappointed that he sat on his haunches and howled for a whole day and a whole night. This made the Karok Indian take pity on him.

"Coyote," said the Karok, "I'll talk to *Chareya* about you. I'll tell him how you tried to win the longest bow."

"Don't forget to tell him how I shook myself to keep awake," Coyote reminded.

"I'll tell him."

"And don't forget to tell him that even though I hate cold water, especially in my ears, I went for a swim in the cold and dark to keep awake."

"I'll tell him," the Karok promised.

"And don't forget that I sang songs — lots of songs, to try to keep awake," urged Coyote.

"I'll tell him everything about you," the Karok said.

The Karok went to talk to *Chareya*. Coyote was so restless that he ran around and around until his tongue was hanging out.

Old Hawk laughed, "Silly! Running around won't help you. Keep still and wait."

But Coyote couldn't keep still. His pride was hurt because he had dreamed of having the longest bow and here he was carrying the very shortest bow of all the animals. He sat down and scratched at his fleas to pass the time until the Karok man would come back. At least, fleas didn't have any bows at all, and that helped his pride a little.

When at last the Karok came back, Coyote leaped to his feet and stood trembling as he waited for the Karok to speak.

"I told *Chareya* everything," Karok reported. "He saw that you were good in some ways even if you are too proud and too eager to be the top animal of all."

"Well, what did he decide?" Coyote asked, his voice squeaking with impatience.

The Karok told Coyote that *Chareya*, after careful thought about Coyote, had decreed that Coyote should become the most crafty and cunning of all animals.

Coyote was so pleased that he threw away his bow.

He was so grateful to the Karok Indians that he made a promise:

"I'll always be your friend and the friend of your children and your children's children. I will do everything I can to help you Karoks."

How Coyote Put Fish in Clear Lake

Pomo Indians living around Clear Lake love Coyote because he gave them fish. Here is the story of the way it happened:

Once long ago a terrible drought came over the land. Indians danced and danced for the Keeper of Rain, but nothing happened. Medicine Men sang chants for rain, but no rain came.

Lakes dried up. Creeks dried up. Rivers dried up.

Hawks flew with beaks open in the hot sun, their throats aching with thirst.

Blue-jays scolded from the tops of sun-scorched trees because there was no water.

Frog's throats were too dry to croak.

Then came more trouble! A great swarm of noisy brown grasshoppers arrived. So many grasshoppers came in a great cloud that they shut off the sun and the sky was dark. They rubbed their wings and feet together and made a "Zing-Zizz" that frightened Indian babies.

Grasshoppers "Zing-zizzed" all over the land and ate up grass so the Indians couldn't collect seeds to grind into mush which they called *too*.

Indian babies cried for food. Indian fathers and mothers went hunting for game and nuts and berries. But the berries and nuts had dried up. Deer had gone away. There were no fishes because lakes and rivers were all dry.

Coyote was roaming the land, hunting for food and just one tiny sip of water for his hot, dry throat.

"If this dryness keeps up and Sun is so hot," said he,

"my whiskers will wither and blow away and my tail will get singed and I'll look a fright."

When he saw the skinny, starving Indians and their hungry babies he forgot about his own troubles. Coyote loved Pomo Indians and their children.

"There must be something to do about dry times — to bring food," he thought. "Great Spirit wouldn't want us all to be thirsty and hungry."

He sat on his haunches one day and looked high into the sky. He looked so high that his neck stretched out six inches longer than it usually was.

Coyote asked Great Spirit: "Please, won't you send us on earth a drink and some food?" And he waited for Great Spirit to whisper the answer back into his big yellow ear.

"Eat grasshoppers," Great Spirit told him. "They're very good to eat, even if they do make brown spots of juice on the grass and keep zizzing all the time."

"Ugh!" Coyote complained, "Grasshoppers don't sound like a good meal to me!"

"Grasshoppers are juicy," Great Spirit whispered back. "You can't tell by just looking at a thing how good it tastes. I sent grasshoppers to earth. I never send anything that cannot be useful one way or another. Eat them and see!"

Coyote shook his head. Grasshoppers looked very hard and bony to him. "They'll scratch all the way down," he grumbled.

"Stop thinking about your own stomach!" Great Spirit said. "You love the Indians. They are hungry and thirsty. You want to help them, don't you?"

Coyote had to admit that the cries of Pomo children kept him awake nights and made his heart ache.

"Then eat grasshoppers for *them*, if not for yourself," Great Spirit told Coyote. "Miracles happen when beings do things they don't want to do—for the sake of others."

Just then Coyote heard the pitiful cry of an Indian boy who was thirsty and hungry.

He took a great breath and held his long nose with one paw, while he grabbed for those zizzing grasshoppers with the other.

Quick, down went those scratchy grasshoppers into his gullet. Coyote gulped a great gulp and swallowed them whole.

They weren't so bad after they were down and they did make his empty stomach feel better, but they scratched and tickled his insides.

"Take more grasshoppers!" Great Spirit urged. "The more you eat the more seeds will grow for Indian mush."

Coyote made a face, took a great breath, and grabbed pawful after pawful of grasshoppers and swallowed them whole until his stomach felt tight.

The grasshoppers did a lot of wiggling inside him. He looked around and found a few more grasshoppers. He thought of Indian children and their hunger for mush—but he just couldn't eat any more grasshoppers.

"I've done the best I can for Indians by eating grasshoppers so that grasshoppers can't keep eating seeds," he told Great Spirit. "I just can't swallow one more."

Great Spirit whispered back to him. "You have done well, Coyote. Never mind the few zizzers that are left. Look over your shoulder now at the dry spot where

Clear Lake used to be."

Coyote was so full of grasshoppers that it was hard to move the least bit. But he wiggled and he groaned and twisted. Finally he managed to look over his left shoulder.

There—in the middle of the dry hole that had once been a lake—was a damp spot, a little bubbling spring!

"Now, go and dig at that spring," Great Spirit told him. "As you dig, more water will come—enough for all Pomo Indians."

"But I can't move!" Coyote complained. "I'm too

full of grasshoppers. They're scratching my stomach."

"Thinking of your stomach again!" Great Spirit said sadly. "You don't love Pomos as much as I thought you did — or you would bestir yourself to bring them water and food."

Just then Coyote heard an Indian baby, Kulot, cry out for food and water.

He thought about that hungry Kulot and forgot his heavy stomach full of grasshoppers. He kept thinking how many people would be helped if he could get to the spring and dig.

So, he slid along on his stomach. He pushed hard with his legs. He strained every muscle in his back and slowly inched nearer and nearer to the little spring.

Whenever Coyote thought of himself he couldn't move. But when he thought of the poor Indians, he could move faster. New strength came to him as if there were a mysterious spring bubbling up inside his own body.

"That's how miracles happen," Great Spirit whispered. "I knew you had a big heart, Coyote—a heart big enough to forget yourself for others."

Coyote was cheered on. He wiggled. He squirmed. He pulled. He pushed with all his might toward the spring.

Finally at sundown, after much wiggling and pushing and squirming, Coyote reached the spring. Feebly, he began to dig.

As he dug with his front paws, strength came into them so he could dig more. Soon water flowed fast in a great stream and he took a drink.

He wanted to run to the Indians and tell them, "I've found *water!*" But his stomach was heavy and he was tired from all the work he had done.

"I must — I *must* go tell the Indians," he groaned. "Poor Pomos need water." He pulled and tugged, but his legs wobbled so he just couldn't run. He could take only one or two steps before he sank down exhausted.

"I see your heartache for the Indians. I will tell them and send them to the water," Great Spirit whispered. "You have done your part well, Coyote."

Soon Indians came to the water — Indian boys and girls and men, and women carrying babies. They all drank and felt better. The ache left Coyote's heart.

When the Indians had gone back to their tule huts and all was quiet, Great Spirit came close to Coyote.

"Now, for the magic." he whispered. "Watch what happens to those few grasshoppers you couldn't eat."

Coyote kept very still and watched. He saw the grasshoppers come to the little shining lake he had dug so Indians could drink. The grasshoppers flew over the lake with a zizzing sound. They saw their reflection in the water. With a quick dart they all jumped into the lake and turned into beautiful shining fishes!

"Now, Coyote, you see what an unselfish heart can do," Great Spirit said tenderly. "It can bring both food and drink to hungry and thirsty people anywhere.

And that is how Coyote started the fish that swim in Clear Lake today.

How the Great Rocks Grew

The Miwok Indians lived in the foothills not far from Yosemite Valley. Miwok means Little Grizzly Bear in our language.

The Miwoks told this story of how two great rocks grew in the Sierra mountains.

Long ago, when Eagle was chief over all, two Miwok boys went swimming with two Miwok girls in a pool.

"This water is warm. We like it," said the girls.

The boys didn't agree with the girls.

"Brrr—this water is cold!" they cried, and shivered. "We're going to sun ourselves on those two nice warm rocks over there."

The rocks warmed by the sun made the boys sleepy. They slept so hard that they didn't even hear the girls laughing and talking nearby.

Then a strange thing happened while those two boys slept. Slowly and silently the rocks began to grow higher and higher.

The day passed and the rocks went on growing taller and taller with the boys on the very top.

The girls were having such a good time in the water they forgot about the two boys who had gone off by themselves.

When sunset came the girls were ready to go back home to the village. They remembered the two boys then and looked for them.

No boys! But where the small rocks and the boys had been were two huge rocks like gray walls that towered up into the clouds.

"Where are you, boys?" the girls called.

No answer came.

They kept on calling and calling, but there was still no answer. Dusk was coming and the girls grew afraid out there alone between those silent, giant rocks.

They ran all the way home to tell their fathers and mothers what had happened.

People from the *Umne*, the Indian village, came down to the river and saw the giant rocks. They realized the boys were up on top hidden by the clouds but they didn't know how to get them down.

They tried and tried to climb up. There was no way to get a fingerhold or a toehold on the smooth walls.

Then Mouse squeaked, "Maybe I can stick my claws in and pull myself up to where the boys are."

"You!" the people sniffed and snuffed, making fun of Mouse. "You're too little."

However, they were afraid for their boys up there, alone and hungry and cold in the dark. They decided to let Mouse try.

Brave little Mouse dug his claws in and tried his hardest. Slowly he pulled himself up, a little at a time. He had gone about as high as a man is tall when his legs grew weak — and then he reached a place where the rock was very slippery.

"Plop!" He came down and landed on the earth below.

The people laughed and Mouse went away to rub his bumped head and body with his sore paws.

"I'm bigger than Mouse," said Rat. "I'll try."

He was a very big fat Rat. He started out well, but soon went "Puff—puff—PUFF."

Soon the "PUFF—PUFFS" came faster and faster. He lost his breath.

"Kerumph!" He fell to earth with a louder thump than Mouse had made. He bared his sharp teeth at the people when he got to his feet, so they didn't dare laugh at him. He went off alone in the dark.

Mountain Lion came up then, without making a sound. "I can jump," he bragged. "I'll jump up and get those boys for you."

Mountain Lion seemed so sure he could jump to the top of the rocks, the people believed maybe he *could* get their boys for them.

"Try—please try," they begged Mountain Lion.

Mountain Lion went off and practiced his springs to limber up his legs.

"Now," he shouted to the people, "get out of the way! I need room to run and spring if you want me to jump high enough to reach those boys."

The people moved away to give Mountain Lion room to run and jump.

He ran, then paused, leaned back on his hind legs, stiffened them suddenly and took a great leap into the air.

He went high on the mountain wall, but he bounced right back like a ball and landed in the river with a loud splash. Wet and cold, he padded silently away into the night, his tail between his legs.

At last Eagle had an idea. "Let's ask Measuring Worm! He is a famous climber."

The people thought Measuring Worm was very small to try to rescue the boys—being only as long as one joint in a finger. But Eagle was chief and had ways of doing things people didn't know about.

Eagle sent first for a sack of money, strings of shell disks called *Humna.* He gave the *Humna* to Dove and sent Dove to get Measuring Worm who lived with his wife in a little house down by the river's edge.

Dove told Measuring Worm about the boys and held out the sack of *Humna.*

"Will you come and rescue them?" Dove asked.

Measuring Worm shook his head in doubt. "I'm too old to try. I'm not as strong as I was when I was young."

"But Eagle says you are famous as a climber," Dove insisted. "Please come."

"Well—I'll come and see," Measuring Worm promised, "but I'm too old."

Dove flew right back. "Measuring Worm is coming!" he called out.

The people stayed there in the dark and waited a long time. Finally Measuring Worm came hobbling slowly along the path, leaning on a stick.

As he came closer, his step was slower and more shaky.

He leaned harder on his cane and stopped for breath. He had a net sack on his back.

Measuring Worm took a long time to look at the rocks and feel them. "They are much too high and too smooth for such an old man to climb," he grumbled. "But I'll try — I'll *try*." His voice sounded very weak and shaky.

Slowly, with trembling hands he tied the carrying net around his waist and started up the nearest rock. As he climbed inch by inch up the rock he sang his own name softly over and over.

"*Honuk-honuk, Honuk-honuk.*"

"Will he be strong enough to reach the top?" the people wondered aloud as the "*Honuk-honuk*" grew fainter and fainter to their ears.

At last Measuring Worm reached the top of one rock and found one of the boys. Over on the rock across the way was the other boy.

"How did you get up here?" he asked the boy beside him.

The boy was too worn out to answer.

The rocks were so far apart that Measuring Worm could not get from one rock to the other. He could take only one boy down at a time.

He spread out his net, put the first boy into it, and slowly climbed down.

"*Honuk-honuk,*" he sang over and over just as he had done coming up.

Finally the people down below heard the song. It grew louder and louder as Measuring Worm came creeping down. The Indians were very happy when he arrived with one boy.

Measuring Worm sat down and fanned himself and fluttered his eyelids and complained of being weary. Then he sighed.

"Now I have to go back after the other boy and I'm tired and old," he grumbled. "But I'll try—I'll *try*."

With that, the father and mother of the boy who was still up on the rock ran home and got a bag of *Humna* and brought it to Measuring Worm. The father and mother of the boy who had been rescued gave him *Humna* too.

After a rest, Measuring Worm started off again singing and inching up the rock. After a long time he came back with the second boy.

The people and the parents of the boys were very grateful to Measuring Worm. They all brought him presents. They gave him more *Humna.* They took turns brushing his back. They tried everything they knew to cure his weakness and lameness.

"You are the only one who was skillful enough to climb the rocks. You saved our boys," they told him.

Measuring Worm put his bag of shell disk money and presents into his net bag and tottered away on his cane —back home to his wife.

When he got out of sight of the people he walked faster. Finally he threw away his cane and walked very fast.

He was not old at all! He just pretended to be old and weak!

He showed his wife all the presents and money and told her how he had brought the boys down in his net.

"All kinds of animals bragged and wanted to bring those boys down," he told her. "I, Measuring Worm, am little but I was the only one who could do it.

The two great rocks that carried the sleepy Indian boys into the sky stand even now in Yosemite Valley.

How Coyote Put Salmon
in the Klamath River

Each year just before the salmon came up the Klamath River, the story teller of the Karok Indians used to call his people together around the campfire. He told them how the salmon, which the Indians called *am*, first came into the river.

Many many moons ago the Great Spirit made the beautiful, shiny, silver salmon and dropped them into the ocean.

"They will be as bright as great stars swimming around in there," the Great Spirit said to himself. "The ocean

will be the blue sky upside down — only more runny —
being water."

Then he put a big dam across the mouth of the Klamath River where it empties into the sea. The dam kept
the sea and the river apart and it was locked by something that looked like a white man's key.

"That will keep my beautiful swimming stars in their
blue ocean until they multiply enough so Indians will
have plenty to eat," the Great Spirit mused. "If I keep
salmon from going up the river, the salmon will grow
faster and have more baby salmon."

Not long after that, the two old hags who had talked
him into giving Fire to their keeping, found out about
the salmon and the dam and the key.

Being greedy hags, they wanted the key.

They rattled their old teeth. They shrieked for the
key until the Great Spirit's ears began to ache.

He shook his head at them.

Those hags kept right on asking. They clattered and
rattled their teeth until the Great Spirit's ears hurt. They
rattled and clattered until he couldn't eat — and he
couldn't sleep!

After they had talked day and night for as many moons
as people have fingers and toes, he finally gave them
the key.

"Here is the key, you bothersome old things," the
Great Spirit told them. "But you must let Indians have
salmon too, enough for the men and women and the
boys and girls. Heads, tails and skins are for skunks and
racoons. All creatures are my children and must be fed."

The old hags promised to give the Indians fish. But

they forgot their promise as soon as they got the key
— just as many people forget their promises before the
next moon comes over the hill.

With their sharp, greedy eyes, the hags kept watch
over the dam night and day. The Indians could never
get near it, for the hags drove them away with their
clubs and their long-nailed fingers. The Indians never
got even a glimpse of the shining silver salmon there
in the river.

Time after time, the hags went down to the dam, un-
locked it with their key, caught some shiny salmon, and
locked the dam again. They walked right past the Indians with the fat salmon. The Indians stood watching,

their dark eyes yearning for the bright, big fish.

The hags went to their hut and cooked the salmon over their fire, on sticks. Licking their lips and clucking their tongues, they picked the salmon to pieces with their bony old fingers. They stuffed themselves and chuckled.

"Gobble," went great chunks down their skinny old throats. They didn't have enough teeth to chew.

A terrible drought came over the land. Seeds were hard to find for Indian mush. Little fishes in the river were all eaten by the hungry Karoks. After that, they didn't know where to find food.

The Indians tried every way they knew to get the old hags to give them some salmon. They begged and pleaded

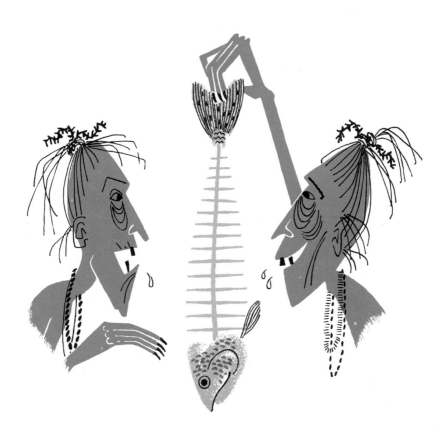

and threatened. The old furies just sniffed and licked their salmon-covered, bony fingers.

Indian children cried because they were so hungry. Indian men went hunting for food and came back empty-handed. Indian women had to tell stories about Frog and Eagle and Hawk, to put courage into the stomachs of their boys and girls, instead of fish and mush from seeds.

Finally, the Karoks were so hungry they went to see Coyote. They told him how hungry they were and that the old hags wouldn't give them a single salmon. They told him all about the dam and the key that the old creatures kept watch of day and night.

"Why didn't you come to me before?" Coyote asked. "I didn't know you at first when I saw you, because your bones stick out where you should look fat. Go back to your lodges. Before another moon I will have every Karok Indian lodge dripping with salmon."

After the Indians had gone, Coyote shook out his tail and started on a journey down to the river.

He trotted for several days, until he came to the river's mouth. Then he saw the big ocean water and heard the noise of great waves pounding on the shore.

He went to the hut where the old hags lived, rapped on the door and asked them to put him up for the night, if they please would be so kind.

The old hag with only four teeth came to the door. She looked at him with her bright old eyes.

"Where have I seen you before?" she asked, scowling.

Coyote wondered if she was thinking of the time he had stolen Fire from her and the other hag.

"Of course you have seen me," he told her slyly and

smiled as wide as his big mouth would open. "You see me in your dreams at night. I come and sing love songs outside your door when the moon is bright."

The old hag had never known the word "love" before. It melted her heart. But being a hag, her hard stony heart didn't melt very much.

Still, Coyote saw that her heart had melted a little bit and he thought again of the starving Indians.

"Don't you remember those sweet high notes?" he asked as softly as a breeze blows. "I sang them especially for you that night last moon ago. Ye—owe—owe." He gave his sweetest howl, so soft and musical that it was almost like a cat's purr. He knew that every woman liked to have a song sung for her alone, even a hag with four teeth. A song for a woman, the Karok men often said, did more than beatings.

The old hag's scowl faded. She almost shaped her crooked mouth into a smile. "Come right in," she invited. "I'm sorry I didn't recognize you before. You have changed some—a little on the leaner side, I think."

Coyote was about to say that he was thin because fish were all gone from the rivers—but something told him not to. The old hags might suspect why he had come to their hut.

He went in and made himself comfortable before the fire, and "Ye—owed" sweetly while he watched the two old hags cook salmon for their supper. He sniffed hungrily, between songs, and his long, pink tongue watered for one taste of fish.

But Coyote's songs were not sweet enough to make the old creatures share their salmon with him.

They just sat on their heels and picked with their fingers and ate. They paid no attention to him licking his lips in hunger for the fine pink meat of the salmon.

All night long, while the hags slept, Coyote lay by the fire singing softly and waiting for the chance to get the mighty key he saw hanging out of reach by the door. Every time he stirred, one of the old hags' bright eyes would pop open.

In the morning, the hag with five teeth took down the key and started off toward the dam to get fish.

Like a flash Coyote leaped in front of her feet. Heels over head she pitched. The key flew far from her hands.

Before she knew what had happened, Coyote had raced to the dam and stood there with the key in his teeth, wrenching at the fastenings.

Finally the fastenings gave way after great tugs that wore all the skin off poor Coyote's paws.

The water "swooshed" through with a great blue roar. With it came hordes of flashing salmon.

The fish were so big and there was so much water, that together they broke the dam wide open!

Ever since then salmon have been swimming up the Klamath River to feed the Indians and their children and their children's children and white men too.

Indians were grateful to Coyote. They built fires in Coyote's honor. They told stories about his great deeds, and his crafty way of getting what he wanted.

When Indian boys did brave deeds, they were called sons of Coyote. When Indian girls were very wise in their ways, they were called the daughters of Coyote.

Why Women Talk More Than Men

Many moons ago, a Shasta Indian man loved a Shasta Indian girl. One day the Shasta Indian man decided that he would tell the Indian girl just how much he loved her.

He spent a long time within his hut of boards and bark and packed earth, under the shadow of great Mt. Shasta, trying to choose the right words to use.

Then one moonlit evening he put on his best buckskin leggings and thrust a bone pin into his long black

hair. He put on his finest *hut-chas*, or moccasins, with their furry bearskin soles. When he was ready, he went out to find the Indian girl.

The Indian girl was dressed in her finest clothes, too. She wore a long, braided apron, and her dark hair was wrapped in two heavy rolls that drooped down in front of her shoulders.

The Shasta man began to whisper into the Shasta girl's ear. He did not want anyone else to hear.

"Your eyes are like the—" For a minute he could not remember the words he had chosen to say. Then he remembered and started over. "Your eyes are like the very darkest pools in the river where the big trout rest."

The girl's dark, bright eyes grew even brighter when she heard this.

"And your hair," the Indian youth whispered, "is as long and black and shining as the crow's wing."

The girl combed at her hair with her fingers, and blushed with pleasure.

"Your mouth," he murmured, "is as red as *kwa-ho-wa*, the sky, when Sun goes down."

The girl smiled and showed her white, small teeth.

"Your teeth," the youth told her, "are whiter than the big snows on top of the mountain."

The girl listened and smiled and blushed. Her red-brown cheeks grew redder. Her bright eyes glistened. It seemed to her that she could go on listening to the beautiful words forever. She thought, "If only my mother and my father and my sister and my brother could hear!"

Suddenly, the Indian man whispered in a rush, "I

love you! I love you so much that I want you to be my wife."

"I love you too!" she cried, but she was too excited to say more. And her ears were singing with all the lovely things the man had told her. She felt that she would burst if she couldn't run and tell all of her relatives. So she turned and went running toward her parents' hut where smoke was curling up through the smoke-hole in the roof.

There, the girl told her mother everything that the youth had whispered to her, even though his words had been meant for her alone when the moon was flowing through the sky.

Then she went and told her father everything that the young man had said.

She told her sister.

She told her brother.

She told all of her friends.

She told everyone, talking as fast as she could: "He said my eyes were like trout pools. My hair like the crow's wing. My mouth like the sky when the red sun goes down. We are going to be married."

Then she went on to tell them all about what she and the Indian man would do when they were married, and about what a wonderful feast there would be.

She dreamed about the new, beautiful words he would whisper to her after they were married.

Finally, there were no more relatives or friends to tell. The Indian girl had got so used to talking that it was hard to stop. Surely there must be someone else she could tell about the Indian youth's whispered words, she thought.

She rushed into the forest. She would tell the animals and the birds!

She found Beaver chewing at a tree trunk by a stream, and she told him.

She found Rabbit nibbling at some sweet, fresh grass, and she told him.

She found Squirrel burying acorns on the mountainside, and she told him.

She even told Mosquito who was just getting ready to push his long stinger into Weasel's back.

She told the birds and the snakes and the fish.

At last, there was no one else to tell.

But now, the girl's mother was busy talking, too. The mother told the Indian youth, himself, what the girl had told her.

The Indian youth said, "But I spoke only for her!"

The girl's father, too, told the Indian young man what the girl had said.

"But I whispered it to her," the Shasta Indian exclaimed, "so that no one else should hear!"

The girl's sister told the Indian man. Then her brother told him. Then the girl's friends told him all over again.

The young Indian man put his hands over his ears as he heard his own words being told back to him. He began to wish that he had never whispered even one word into the Shasta girl's ear.

At last, he could stand all the chatter no longer. He put on his old deerskin leggings and his old, shabby moccasins, and fled to the forest. He did not bother to put a bone pin in his black hair, this time.

But when he got to the forest, the animals there began bleating and barking and yowling about what the girl had told them. The birds chirped and sang about it. Mosquito hummed on and on about all the girl had told.

The Indian pressed his hands to his ears and cried, "Stop! Stop! I don't want to hear any more about it."

Magpie, who was the worst chatterer of all, settled herself in a low branch of a tree and chattered right on. Magpie fluttered her black and white wings and gave a shrill, cackling laugh at the Indian lover.

"Garrack!" Magpie mocked in her croaking voice. "So you think her eyes are like dark pools in the river, do you?"

"Hush!" the man begged. "I've heard enough about what I said."

Magpie went right on chattering and laughing. Her beak clacked faster and faster.

"Garrack!" Magpie taunted. "Her hair is as long and black and shining as a crow's wing."

"Quiet!" the Indian pleaded. He pressed his hands tighter against his ears.

But Magpie was enjoying herself so much that her beak clacked even faster and her voice got shriller and louder. The whole woods echoed with her harsh voice.

"And her mouth," Magpie screeched, "is as red as the sky when the red sun goes down! You love her! You want her for your wife!"

The Indian youth could stand no more. He trembled with rage. He clenched his fist and shook it at Magpie.

"A curse on you all—women and magpies!" he shouted. He turned, fleeing from the forest, and muttering to himself, "Every woman is a magpie. She can't keep her mouth shut."

As he ran, he promised himself he would never tell any woman anything again—no matter how black her hair might be, or how red her mouth.

He did not stop running until he came to the river. There he made himself a tule boat, paddled off and was never heard from again.

But the curse put on women and magpies is still strong. That is why, Shasta Indians say, women talk more than men.